T0395388

Shapes and Patterns in Nature

THIS EDITION
Editorial Management by Oriel Square
Produced for DK by WonderLab Group LLC
Jennifer Emmett, Erica Green, Kate Hale, *Founders*

Editors Grace Hill Smith, Libby Romero, Maya Myers, Michaela Weglinski;
Photography Editors Kelley Miller, Annette Kiesow, Nicole DiMella;
Managing Editor Rachel Houghton; **Designers** Project Design Company;
Researcher Michelle Harris; **Copy Editor** Lori Merritt; **Indexer** Connie Binder; **Proofreader** Larry Shea;
Reading Specialist Dr. Jennifer Albro; **Curriculum Specialist** Elaine Larson

Published in the United States by DK Publishing
1745 Broadway, 20th Floor, New York, NY 10019

Copyright © 2023 Dorling Kindersley Limited
DK, a Division of Penguin Random House LLC
23 24 25 26 10 9 8 7 6 5 4 3 2 1
001-334088-July/2023

A catalog record for this book
is available from the Library of Congress.
HC ISBN: 978-0-7440-7445-1
PB ISBN: 978-0-7440-7446-8

DK books are available at special discounts when purchased in bulk for sales promotions, premiums, fundraising, or educational use. For details, contact: DK Publishing Special Markets,
1745 Broadway, 20th Floor, New York, NY 10019
SpecialSales@dk.com

Printed and bound in China

The publisher would like to thank the following for their kind permission to reproduce their images:
a=above; c=center; b=below; l=left; r=right; t=top; b/g=background

123RF.com: Petra Schüller / pixelelfe 24bc; **Dorling Kindersley:** Blackpool Zoo, Lancashire, UK 21bl;
Dreamstime.com: Alexma<72427 4-5, Andreykuzmin 18-19, 31cl, Antares614 6-7, 31cla, Valentin M Armianu 9br, Justin Black 1bc, Radu Cadar 26-27, Chaoticmind 19br, Chuyu 25bl, Coconutdreams 24-25, 31bl, Paulo Cruz 26br, Sandi Cullifer 27br, Benoit Daoust 10-11, 31clb, Deosum 6br, Jackie Egginton 11br, Fallsview 9bl, Oleg Gerasymenko 30, Golfxx 3cb, Gordzam 23cb, Icmway 14-15, Virender Jaiswal 12br, Natthakan Jommanee 17bl, Matthijs Kuijpers 22-23, Brian Kushner 28-29, Fabio Lamanna 19bc, Puripat Lertpunyaroj 12-13, Lilkar 29br, Mihalcin 23br, Ninelroschina 13br, Matee Nuserm 28bc, Onionastudio 7br, Olga Popova 16bc, Ravindu Praveen 27bc, Rusel1981 18br, Saknakorn 14ca, Seadam 16-17, Yali Shi 10bc, Slew11 8bc, Taweesak Sriwannawit 21bc, Mikhail Strogalev 17br, Sufi70 11bl, Susazoom 14br, Thomas Vieth 15bl, Waj111 13bc, Wrangel 22bc, Znm 4bl, 20-21; **Getty Images:** Stone / Manoj Shah 29bc;
Getty Images / iStock: Peerajit 20bc, wsfurlan 7cb; **Shutterstock.com:** MRacheron 8-9, 31tl, ON-Photography Germany 4c

Cover images: *Front:* **Dreamstime.com:** Dannyphoto80, Anna Velichkovsky cb; **Shutterstock.com:** KOSTENKO b;
Back: **Dreamstime.com:** Vertyr cla; **Getty Images / iStock:** KristinaVelickovic clb; **Shutterstock.com:** IgorMass cra

All other images © Dorling Kindersley
For more information see: www.dkimages.com

For the curious
www.dk.com

Shapes and Patterns in Nature

Libby Romero

Nature has many shapes and patterns.

Rain makes circles on a lake.

circles

A rainbow is an arch in the sky.

arches

Many eggs are shaped like ovals.

ovals

Some volcanoes are shaped like triangles.

triangles

You can find heart shapes in nature.

hearts

You can find star shapes.

stars

There are hexagons, too.

hexagons

Shapes repeat.
They make patterns.
Look at these stripes.

stripes

21

Look at these spots.

spots

23

spirals

Look at these spirals.

Look at the seeds.
See the pattern.

patterns

wings

Look at the pattern
on these wings.
One side is like
the other.

We see shapes and patterns every day!

Glossary

arch
something with
a curved shape

circle
a round shape with
no corners or straight
edges

hexagon
a flat shape with six
angles and six sides

oval
a shape like a circle that
is longer than it is wide

spiral
a curve that winds
around a fixed point

Quiz

Answer the questions to see what you have learned. Check your answers with an adult.

1. What shape do raindrops make when they fall on water?

2. What shape are some volcanoes?

3. How many sides does a hexagon have?

4. What pattern is on a zebra?

5. What is your favorite shape or pattern? Where can you find that shape or pattern in nature?

1. Circles 2. Triangles 3. Six 4. Stripes 5. Answers will vary